HOW TO LIVE IN THE OVERFLOW

A FUNDAMENTAL APPROACH TO KINGDOM WEALTH!

By Renee Rainey

RnR Investment Company, LLC

Living in the Overflow: A Fundamental Approach to Kingdom Wealth!

Your Free Gift

I have included in this eBook a Business Plan outline.
http://www.videomarketingforprofits.com/

TABLE OF CONTENTS

WHY I WROTE THIS BOOK

Yes, it was fun to do. But most importantly living in the Overflow is a powerful place to be. It will make you strong financially, you'll have negotiating power. You'll be a lender and not a borrower. The reason I wrote this book is because I am a single woman with dreams to become wealthy one day. Initially, I had no prior financial education, mentors or a strategy to get there. I had to take the initiative to self-educate my own. So if I could do it so can you. I'm here to take you on a journey to becoming financially free. Living debt-free is an achievable lifestyle. It's not an overnight fix and not just to get out of debt short-term. It's a great everyday way to get to your desired lifestyle.

Why You Should Read This Book

If you commit to the basic principles and stick to your plans, here are some of the positive results you might expect:

- Better sleep
- Negotiating power
- Less stress
- Cash in the bank
- Money to Invest
- Major/Minor Purchases with Cash

CHAPTER 1

For the first 6 years of my life I lived with both parents until they divorced. Both parents worked full time jobs and I wanted for nothing, had the best of material things and was provided for. My mom later moved my sister and I to Pittsburgh, PA. There in Pennsylvania was my first encounter with poverty and lack, low income housing, and roaches. I lived with my mom until the age of 10 or 11 and then I went to live with my dad until young adulthood. My dad worked for General Motors with a great benefit package, standard of living was better with my dad. My parents never discussed or educated me on finances or debt. I learned the hard way about money before I got financially smart.

"Deut.15:6 Thou shalt lend to many nations, but thou shalt not borrow."

I remember the first credit cards that I applied for with a $1,000 limit, I could choose between a MasterCard or Visa or both, so I choose both. I was naïve and thought I had $1000.00 per card instead I only had $1000.00 totaled between the two cards. Being young and dumb I never read the contract that came with the cards. This lead me to my first embarrassing moment. While out shopping for clothes one day my card was declined. I was perplexed and wondered how it could be happening to me. I had never used my second card before? I demanded that they put MasterCard on the phone only for them to deliver the news that I could not make my purchases due to being over my limit. My source of funds were dried up that day, I was using my credit card like that was available money to use for what my paycheck could not buy. I never realized that I was borrowing money and had to pay the piper back with interests. Of course I made the minimum payments that the statement requested and I did not know about paying in full instead. So that dress on sell ended up being sale price plus interest. That was my red flag. It was time for a financial intervention. It was time to ask someone for help, time to educate myself on credit and debt and stay out for good. The message did not become clear until after several attempts. I was in debt way over my head that finally in my late forties did a light bulb go off and I embraced the fact that credit cards are not for me personally and it was keeping me in bondage.

Credit cards are a money makers for financial institutions.

Read more: http://www.creditcards.com/credit-card-news/credit-card-industry-facts-personal-debt-statistics-1276.php#ixzz2lDUb76mX

"Proverb 22:7 "The poor are always ruled over by the rich, so don't put yourself under their power." (MSG)"

CHAPTER 2

I was making six figures when I owned my first salon. I wanted to retire at age 30; I was disappointed when that did not happen. When I started my own business back in 1987 I was still young and dumb financially but full of faith and ambition. I did not have a plan or strategy to retire at an early age. I moved to Ohio January 1997, I found a church that I had to be a part of. I sold my lucrative business, got a $5,000 loan, and loaded up the U-Haul. Three months after moving to Ohio my hair clientele had not picked up quick enough to pay for my new mortgage, my car payment, my loan back home, and my new credit card debts that I had acquired. I had to find employment. I found a corporate job making a little over $10.00 an hour. Oh Lord, is this a curse??? I had decided that I would give the corporate job at least 5 years. That job lasted for 16 years, I eventually despised my job. I felt trapped on a job that I didn't like and had it in my mind that I had to stay just to pay off old debt and pay off new accumulated debt. See how a person life can spiral out of control? When you are in a ditch do you keep digging? God forbid!

I turned the situation around to my advantage. I utilized the matching 401k plan, took advantage of the tuition reimbursement program, the commission and bonus programs, and worked all the overtime that was offered. I saved my annual company stocks instead of cashing them in. I purchased saving bonds that was auto drafted directly from my check. I was well on my way. The first couple of years it was rough, I didn't make enough money to meet my increasing variable mortgage, condo fees and bills. I got behind in my bills and saw no way out of the rat race. I didn't want to face my reality; I would hibernate in my home and not answer the phone to avoid bill collectors. I then got pregnant with my daughter Rashauna. The day I bought her home from the hospital was a turning point for me financially. I heard a knock on the door and it was AEP the light company, I answered with my new born baby girl in my arms. He said, "Miss Rainey I am here to cut your lights off if you would just give me a check I will not precede with the disconnection." I gave him a check, not one of those faith checks we sometimes give that we write and pray that it doesn't bounce. It was that day I decided enough was enough, I need to make a change in my life and it starts today.

CHAPTER 3

Here are choice and mindset changes that I made to improve my financial future. I decided that I would always provide a safe and secured environment for my daughter. I would stop digging myself further into a debt hole and pay cash for purchases. I would stop borrowing money from credit cards and stop using companies account that offered 90 day same as cash. I decided that I would never have another broke day again! I do not allow my savings account to go below a certain amount.

I had to create a strategy to accomplish my financial goals and here are the steps that I used to get out of debt. Fill free to customize your journey.

- My tithes 10% to my local church. It could be to your favorite charity. "**Malachi 3:10 Bring all the tithes into the storehouse.**"

- Pay myself 10% in the early days I could not do 10% I started out with $25.00 a pay. Start where you are. Don't touch it be patient it will grow! "**Proverb 21:20 There is a treasure to be desired and oil in the dwelling of the wise; but a foolish man spendeth it up.**"

- Make a budget and stick to it. Cut out luxuries items until you have an overflow to pay for it. Be creative in generating extra funds for your wants. Find something to sell around the house on Craigslist or have a garage sale. It's cheaper to cook your own meals verses eating out. Re-evaluate your circle of friends if they are all broke and demonstrate the habits you are trying to get away from find new friends. Don't let your broke friends discourage or distract you from your goals of getting out of debt. They are the ones that will come and borrow money from you and not pay you back. You can still enjoy life. I found ways to save money on expenses. I did my own hair and nails, became an expert at mixing and matching my existing wardrobe. I purchased my daughters clothes at consignment shops and traded them back in for the new purchases. To be honest that's when she wore designer clothes.

- I pulled my credit report and faced the truth about my status head on.

  o Expreian-1-888-397-3742
       Website: www.experian.com

- o Equifax- 1-800-685-1111
     Website: www.equifax.com

- o Transunion Credit Bureau- 1-877-322-8228 Website: www.transunion.com

- o You can obtain a free credit report

- I went to Consumer Credit Counselors and they put me on a budget and made arrangements with my creditors until they were paid back in full. It took me 2 ½ years. Pay your bills on time! You can do this yourself as well as for free. (I've included a letter to send to your creditors.) **"Romans 13:8 Don't run up debts, except for the huge debt of love you owe each other."**

- I lowered my bills by removing the highly priced combination packages for the basics services. No movies channels for me or fully loaded new vehicles. I'll buy a fully loaded used vehicle for a reduced price.

- Times when I would get a raise or an extra bonus check, instead of increasing my spending I would increase my savings or investments and continue to live off my current income.

CHAPTER 4

I was a facilitator at my church for Dave Ramsey Financial Peace University through my church. The course is made up of six steps:

Step 1~ Put $1,000 in an emergency fund. The $1,000 it is for the unexpected emergencies that sometime sneak up on us. If your washer or dryer breaks down or the car needs tires you are prepared.

Step 2~ Pay off all debt except the house utilizing the debt snowball the subject was on ways of getting out of debt.

Step 3~ Three to six months of expenses in savings

Step 4~ Invest 15% of your household income into Roth IRAs and pre-tax retirement plans

Step 5~ College funding

Step 6~ Pay off your home early

Step 7~ Build wealth and give!

I added a couple of my own steps:

Step 8~ Create passive income, write books, create on-line courses, create your own products

Step 9~ Start businesses that can run successfully without you

If you are interested in a Dave Ramsey Financial course near you visit www.daveramsey.com

I have found that people are unhappy with their financial situation, but are unwilling to make the necessary changes to become financially free. When I was facilitating Financial Peace at my church when it came time to put the steps in to action I received excuses. Dave Ramsey step 1 encourages you to fund your emergency fund starting with $1,000. Everyone was in agreement with the teaching but no one did it. When we got to the lesson on cutting up our credit cards and paying off the balances I was the only one who did it out of a group of thirty people. The people gave excuses why they could not and would not cut up their cards and why they needed to hold on to their cards. One person's excuse was to hold on to the card for emergencies, another person's was my frequent flyer miles are important, and/or just fearful to cut them up. This was the first time I cut up my credit cards by choice and not because my accounts were closed by the card company. Prior times I would pay off my debt wait a few years and then reapply for a new card and not correct my bad habits. I have since contacted the credit bureau and had them take my name off of the marketing list for credit cards.

Dave's philosophy is to save up for the things you want to buy, pay cash, including the purchase of a car. We are living in a society where we can get instant credit, buy now and pay later or 90 days same as cash.

Credit Card Crumbs (From Dave Ramsey Financial Peace University)

- The total American Consumer debt is more than $2.7 trillion.

- The average household credit card debt has increased approximately 167% in the past 17 years.

- There are over 1.3 billion credit cards in circulation in America

- The credit card industry mails out over six billion credit card offers each year, sending an average of six offers a month to each American household.

- 45% of American cardholders make only the minimum payments on their consumer debt.

- The average balance per credit card-holding is more than $9,300

- A single, offense late payment can immediately raise a cardholder's interest rate as high as 34%.

- The credit card industry takes in $43 billion per year in additional, unexpected income from consumers in fees, such as late payments, over-the-limit, and balance transfer.

Due to the facts on credit card debt it explains where our extra money goes. For me it was my vacation money, my daughter's college tuition and any other heart's desire that I had. I am a strong believer that God blesses and trust us with more than what we need but we squander the money and fail at being good financial stewards. The enemy's' job is to kill, steal and destroy from the believer and we fall into the financial traps of the enemy. I can tell you from experience of spending money without emergency money, it will comes back to haunt you. The lender will call in the debt when we least expect it and catch us unaware and unprepared. Financing your luxury items is a false foundation to build your house upon. When the storms of life happen, and you have a strong financial foundation you will be prepared to weather the storms. Take back control over your finances and you will be a winner! If you are want to get out of debt and find the nearest Financial Peace University please visit fpuonline.com.

CHAPTER 5

Building a Portfolio

I went to some banking institutions to inquire on how to build my portfolio to no avail they could not help me without first having $10,000. I did not have that amount in cash. I headed to the library and found some books to help me grow financially. I read books by Robert and Kim Kiyosaki "Rich dad Poor dad" and their advisors, "Real Estate Investing" Neapolitans Hill "Think and Grow Rich", William O'Neil Successful Investor. The books were easy to understand and follow, I decided that I didn't want to be an outsider looking in I want to be an insider looking out. I am not going to spend a lot of time trying to create the wheel when someone else has already created a successful businesses template. I am going to research and join those that are doing what I want to and do what they are doing. They became my mentors/coaches!

I believe in multiple streams of income. Many financial planners preach to diversify your portfolio, if all of your investments are stock related and if the market crashes there goes your whole portfolio up in smoke.

"Ecclesiastes 11:1-2 Cast thy bread upon the waters: for thou shalt find it after many days. 2. Give a portion to seven and also to eight; for thou knowest not what evil shall be upon the earth."

- I took action steps I started a savings account I put money in it every pay. (could be as low as $25.00)

- I took advantage of my jobs 401k matching Plan.

- I joined an investment club of about 8 women we buy and sell stocks. We have invested in Vacation Property in Brazil.

- I've purchased Government Savings Bonds.

- I had a mutual fund which is now an IRA.

- I've purchased Rental Investment Property.

- I've opened an on-line brokerage account and purchased stock.

- I've started a business.

- I've created intellectual property and have mad passive income (This book)

- Joined companies Affiliate programs

- Accumulated Gold and Silver bars in monthly increments. If you are interested in including Gold or Silver into your portfolio feel free to sign-up under this link **http://www.karatbars.com/?s=rainey04**

If there is ever a time which I believe is very soon, our currency will hold no value. I have traveled to other countries where they do not except the American dollar. I have found that gold and silver is still a universal currency. You can buy and sell in just about any place in the world. So I have started systematically purchasing Gold bars in small quantities. It is very easy to convert gold to cash.

I have an online brockage account where I buy and sell stock. I use the Can-slim method. I have learned through using their system that I am a wiser investor. One strategy that I use I set perimeters if my stock drops 5-8% I sell it, if it goes up to 20% it is still as strong or stronger then the day I purchase it I then decide to purchase more shares or hold on for the long ride up the charts. If it's not showing signs of growth I pull out and take my 20% profit. I have down a full series on YouTube on how to select winning stocks.

- https://www.youtube.com/watch?v=fHcW G6VbIHU

- https://www.youtube.com/watch?v=HPbV QJfyUSc

- https://www.youtube.com/watch?v=MZB0 ogHEu_4

- https://www.youtube.com/watch?v=aNvPV SRj5pw

I decided that real estate rental income was the best fit for my portfolio. Real estate offers both tax advantages and advantages of appreciation, the tendency of a property to increase in value overtime. I took the Real Estate Investment 6 week course with Robert Kiyosaki and was assigned a coach. The course was intense and within six weeks my coach and I had gone through all of the 6 steps to Becoming a Successful Real Estate Investor.

1. I had to create a team of professionals an attorney, an accountant, a real estate agent, and a mortgage broker all who also owned real estate properties.

2. Made sure I was financially ready to make the purchase.

3. Set my real estate goals

4. Found my first investment property, a duplex. Look for properties in areas that are up and coming with good schools. Location! Location ! Location!

5. Analyze the Property Forma. One unit paid the mortgage and expenses, and the other unit was passive income

6. Negotiate with the seller. Most Investor indicates that you make your profit at the negotiation table.

7. Closed on my first property! It was a duplex.

   If you want to take the course visit richdadcoaching.com

CHAPTER 6

Business Plan

I hold my real estate business entity under a LLC. The purpose that I am setting up the real estate business is because I want to leave a legacy to my daughter. The LLC is a way to transfer wealth to my daughter and if she chooses she can pass this business to her children. Here is a Questionnaire and when you answer the questions it will give you a great start to your business plan.

Write a Business Plan *Habakkuk 2:2 Write the vision, and make it plain upon tables, that he may run that readeth it.*

Answer these questions to give you a start to your business plan

Why are we necessary? Define the problem we solve or the need/want we satisfy. Identify the audience who has the need.

What do we do? Describe the nature of our product/service in terms of the benefit we provide our target market.

Who are we? Characterize our personnel, their habits, experience, core competencies and core values. Attach an organization chart as it will look in 3 years, giving current staff multiple roles.

Who do we serve? Be very specific in describing our target market and what characteristic(s) they have that create their need for our solution(s). Describe our areas of sub-specialization, if necessary.

Also, specify the type of business/customers we do not seek.

How and where do we find those we serve? Describe the methods, channels and relationships we use to promote, sell and deliver our product/services.

How are we unique? To _____ (target customer segment), _____ (product/ services name) is the only _____ (product/ services category) that _____ (benefit) because _____ (reason to believe benefit claim). Unlike _____ (competitors), we _____ (differentiation).

Where are we going? State our overall vision/purpose. Use an ambitious goal. Make it something the whole staff can find meaningful and embrace. Then, narrow to a 3-5 year mission statement. Cite milestones (some financial, some non-financial) that represent successful future performance.

WHAT WE NEED TO DO GET THERE? LIST THE RESOURCES (E.G., STAFF, EQUIPMENT, FACILITIES, CAPITAL, RELATIONSHIPS) WE NEED TO EXECUTE OUR PLAN.

HOW DO WE STAY ON COURSE? BRIEFLY DESCRIBE THE MAJOR PROCESSES/SYSTEMS (E.G. CONTACT MANAGEMENT, ORDER PROCESSING, PURCHASING & INVENTORY CONTROL, PRODUCTION, JOB MANAGEMENT, CUSTOMER SERVICE) WE WILL USE TO OPERATE AND CONTROL THE BUSINESS.

Roadblocks: List our 3 toughest obstacles and our maneuvers to surpass them:

What are the Roadblocks?	*How do we overcome these obstacles?*

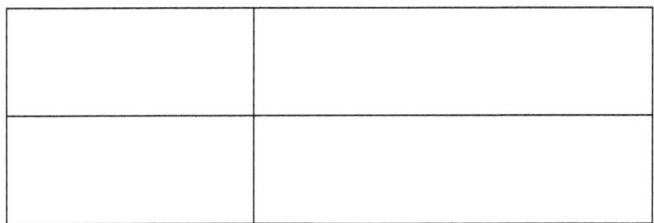

Why do we do what we do? Specify the rewards the team will reap from this undertaking (e.g., financial, career development, and enjoyment).

Use Business Questionnaire from CDC Small Business Development

CHAPTER 7

Children/Teen Portfolio

I have an awesome teenage daughter Rashauna. I am able to teach her at a young age about money and finances. Get your children involved. When you send your young adult off to college many are in debt after college that takes many years to pay back. When she was born instead of buying all the unnecessary baby gadgets I requested family members and friends to buy savings bonds for the first 3 years of her life. I opened a savings account in her name. I taught her the same principles I use 10% to God, 10% in her savings and the rest is for her spending. When she turned 12 years old, I gave her a folder filled with the companies that she knew and recognized. I opened an online brokerage account in her name gave her $100.00 and let her pick the stock from the folder that she wanted to buy. It is a custodian account. It was after the 9/11 stock market crash and some quality companies were on sale. She did very well she tripled her money. She is better at selecting stock than her mother. Rashauna has started her own business *Rashauna's Natural Blends*. She makes organic body butters, lip balms and organic shampoos and conditioners and has a growing customer base. She also has a creative side she puts designs on t-shirts and denim jackets, and she has made jewelry. When I quit my job and she needed school clothes she looked around the house and sold items that were collecting dust and raised the money. When I started my Real Estate business, she was right there with me during the property search, bank and people transactions, dealing with tenants the good and the bad.

<u>Leaving</u>

I want to   a legacy
like my fa   My dad
passed away a couple of years ago. I had a dream one day that my father had passed away and I could not

find his important paperwork true story; I called him and told him to tell me where all his paperwork was located. At that time my dad briefly told me that he wanted my sister and I to split everything 50/50. My dad had remarried and divorced and wanted his former wife to have nothing. I told my dad to have everything in writing because I knew that I would not fight over small things like furniture. My dad was adamant that his ex-wife would get nothing. My dad went as far as to have an attorney put his request in writing. I am proud of my dad he did not leave a trail of debt behind for my sister and me to clean up. Instead he left behind a legacy that keeps on giving to my sister and me month after month. My grandfather was a business man and owned land in South Carolina over 100 acres. My grandfather used the land for farming, he grew cotton and tobacco. Once his eleven children moved away, he had a small store with a kitchen on the land. He would make sandwiches for the factory workers across the street. Over the years the family sold off some of the land. That land was passed down to my dad and his siblings and we obtained his portion when he passed. So I plan to follow his lead. It will be my pleasure to pass my possessions on to my daughter. I have been grooming her to carry on the torch after I'm gone. The transfer of wealth will not be foreign to her. God is good!

In Conclusion

My financial journey is still in progress I am still growing my portfolio and teaching my daughter to do the same. The sky is the limit, be willing to stretch yourself and expand your borders. Don't limit yourself to just my steps or the strategies that I use. I have found as I grew in knowledge I grew in different processes. Allow yourself to use new tools and grow and process at your own personal growth. It is one step at a time it doesn't happen overnight but know that it will happen eventually. If you make a mistake along the way use that as a learning experience and a stepping stone and not give in to defeat. I hope that this was helpful to you and much success to you on your financial journey to financial freedom.

HERE IS MY BOOK LIST THAT HELPED IN MY EDUCATION:

Think and grow rich http://amzn.to/1MdhWw7

Financial Peace University http://amzn.to/1Ph6Mvy

Rich Dad Poor Dad http://amzn.to/1Mdi3HQ

Silver and God http://amzn.to/1MdhY7e

Money Master the Game: 7 Simple Steps to Financial Freedom http://amzn.to/1hp9Ac8

How to Make Money in the Stocks http://amzn.to/1P3ByJb

The ABC's of Real Estate Investing http://amzn.to/1LlTYlO

CONNECT WITH RENEE

Thank you so much for taking time to read this book! I'm so excited for you to start your journey on becoming Financially Free. The way to contact me to connect is through my

Facebook Page http://facebook.com/reneerainey

Twitter http://twitter.com/rnrinvest.

I am active on those platforms throughout the day. You can send me a personal email to reneehairweavingstudio@gmail.com. If you are looking for a way to say thanks, please send me a note on my thank you page http://thankyoutina.com/ or leave me a personal voicemail message https://www.speakpipe.com/sparkwisdom.

ABOUT THE AUTHOR

Hello my name is Renee; I call myself "The Beginners Beginning Financial Coach". I am a single mother that had to take control over my financial future. I am not a professional financial planner, although it's just a matter of going to take a test and becoming certified. I have enough education, personal experience, invested time, research and a strong mentor background to assist in getting you started in the right direction with creating a sound portfolio that is profitable.

I own multiple businesses, RnR Investment Company, LLC and Renee's Hair-weaving Studio, LLC. I have a Bachelor Degree in Business Administration, and an Associate Degree in Small Business Management. While pursuing my Bachelor

Degree in business I detoured occasionally in finance classes all but finished an Associate Degree in Finance (2 classes shy). I am an educator, I am a facilitator for Dave Ramsey (Financial Peace University), and I have completed the Real Estate Investment course for Richdad/Poordad.

ONE LAST THING

Thank you for reading this book! If you enjoyed it found the information useful and especially if you used the information to produce results please post a short 2-3 sentence review on Amazon or if you are into video marketing like me, post a video review and include it on Amazon and YouTube too. I would appreciate it so much. Your support really does make a difference and I read all the reviews personally so I can get your feedback and make this book even better.

If you'd like to leave a review then all you need to do is leave it on Amazon and the link is simple to remember –

Your review link here (be sure to publish the book on Amazon FIRST to get the review link)

That's it.

Thank you so much and let's grow great together!